"Brief, insightfu[l] ... deserves wide ci[rculation]"

 Peter J. Wi[lliams,] Principal, Tyndale House, Cambridge

"This concise, biblically sound book packs a powerful punch. It is a much-needed and edifying resource for the church in view of the world's misapprehensions about Christianity. I highly recommend it."

 Becket Cook, author, *A Change of Affection: A Gay Man's Incredible Story of Redemption*; Host, *The Becket Cook Show*

"Sharon James has written a critical book for a critical time. With characteristic intellectual rigor and concrete evidence, she makes an overwhelming case for the positive impact of Christianity on the world, both historically and today. But what makes this book really stand out is how clear, concise, and easy to read it is. It is well worth anyone's time!"

 Philippa Taylor, Director, Institute for Faith and Culture

"A vital read in our cultural moment, giving us renewed courage to see that authentic discipleship leads to the transformation of society for human flourishing, as we ourselves have been transformed by the self-giving God."

 Benedict Harding, Head of Relay and Leadership Network, UCCF: The Christian Unions

"The gospel is a simple, glorious message that has radically changed the world. Seeds of truth have brought forth beauty. It can be disappointing, therefore, when the massive contributions of the Christian gospel are neglected in the minds of the majority of those who benefit from it daily. Sharon James has written a uniquely powerful and clear book, demonstrating historically, sociologically, and with excellent examples that Christianity has been good for the world—and still is."

Ben Virgo, Director, Christian Heritage London

"Sharon James is a gift to Christ's church. This clear and concise book will help Christians and non-Christians see that freedom, dignity, justice, education, technology, creation care, and hospitals did not arise in a vacuum. They grew from the soil of the Christian worldview. James shows the beauty of the ways of God and how the gospel is, in fact, good news for the whole world."

Blake White, Lead Pastor, South Side Baptist Church, Abilene, Texas

Is Christianity Good for the World?

TGC Hard Questions

Jared Kennedy, Series Editor

Does God Care about Gender Identity?, Samuel D. Ferguson

Is Christianity Good for the World?, Sharon James

Why Do We Feel Lonely at Church?, Jeremy Linneman

Is Christianity Good
for the World?

Sharon James

:: CROSSWAY®

WHEATON, ILLINOIS

Is Christianity Good for the World?

Copyright © 2023 by Sharon James

Published by Crossway
        1300 Crescent Street
        Wheaton, Illinois 60187

Portions of this booklet build on, and refer to, Sharon James, *How Christianity Transformed the World* (Fearn, Ross-shire, UK: Christian Focus, 2021); *The Lies We Are Told: The Truth We Must Hold* (Fearn, Ross-shire, UK: Christian Focus, 2022); and *A Student's Guide to Worldview* (Fearn, Ross-shire, UK: Christian Focus, 2022); in addition to articles by James published in the Affinity *Social Issues Bulletin*, vols. 43–47 (https://www.affinity.org.uk/bulletin) and on the Christian Institute website (https://www.christian.org.uk/features/).

Cover design: Ben Stafford

Cover images: Unsplash, StreetWill

First printing 2023

Printed in the United States of America

Scripture quotations are from the ESV® Bible (The Holy Bible, English Standard Version®), copyright © 2001 by Crossway, a publishing ministry of Good News Publishers. Used by permission. All rights reserved. The ESV text may not be quoted in any publication made available to the public by a Creative Commons license. The ESV may not be translated into any other language.

Trade paperback ISBN: 978-1-4335-9175-4
ePub ISBN: 978-1-4335-9177-8
PDF ISBN: 978-1-4335-9176-1

Library of Congress Cataloging-in-Publication Data

Names: James, Sharon, 1959– author.
Title: Is Christianity good for the world? / Sharon James.
Description: Wheaton, Illinois : Crossway, 2023. | Series: TGC hard questions | Includes bibliographical references and index.
Identifiers: LCCN 2023002731 (print) | LCCN 2023002732 (ebook) | ISBN 9781433591754 (trade paperback) | ISBN 9781433591761 (pdf) | ISBN 9781433591778 (epub)
Subjects: LCSH: Christian sociology. | Christianity and politics—History. | Church and social problems—History. | Persecution—History. | Freedom of religion—History.
Classification: LCC BT738 .J35 2023 (print) | LCC BT738 (ebook) | DDC 261.8—dc23/eng/20230527
LC record available at https://lccn.loc.gov/2023002731
LC ebook record available at https://lccn.loc.gov/2023002732

Crossway is a publishing ministry of Good News Publishers.

BP		32	31	30	29	28	27	26	25	24	23
15	14	13	12	11	10	9	8	7	6	5	4	3	2	1

Contents

Is Christianity Good for the World?   *1*

Notes   *41*

Recommended Resources   *57*

Scripture Index   *59*

"I'M DONE WITH CHRISTIANITY!" Sophie exclaimed.

Through her tears, she explained that a pastor she'd formerly respected had been found guilty of abuse. How had she been fooled into thinking he was a good man? Surely this proved Christians are hypocrites! Her college friends had long told her that Christianity is terrible for women. Maybe they were right.

Sophie isn't alone. A quarter of Generation Z teens say hypocrisy among Christians is a barrier to believing in God.[1]

Sophie was right to be angry. All abuse is evil. It's even more outrageous when a person in a position of trust abuses that trust. Sadly, throughout history abuse has taken place and continues to today. Sometimes it's wrongly perpetrated in the name of Christ. But nominal, institutional religion must be distinguished from real, living Christianity. Jesus Christ strongly condemned religious leaders, and others, who hurt those in their care (Matt. 18:6). The Bible also warns of "wolves in sheep's clothing," and it tells us we are to judge the reality of someone's profession of faith *not* by fine words (or great preaching) but by what they *do*. "You will recognize them by their fruits" (Matt. 7:16).

But when we're tempted to reject all Christians as hypocrites, or the faith as dangerous and oppressive, we need to remember that the ideals of justice, freedom, and compassion are *all* based on the biblical worldview. Indeed, the fact that Sophie and so many others are outraged by abuse is the outworking of that worldview.

A growing number of commentators admit this. Tom Holland, for example, author of *Dominion: The Making of the Western Mind*, believed as a youth that Christianity had ushered in an age of superstition, and that the Enlightenment revived classical values.[2] When he studied Christianity's effects on Western civilization, he discovered that the self-giving example of Christ and the Christian ethic that respects all human life as made in God's image are the *real* foundation of *all* those values we cherish.[3] He writes:

> [Christianity] is the principal reason why, by and large, most of us who live in post-Christian so-

cieties still take for granted that it is nobler to suffer than to inflict suffering. It is why we generally assume that every human life is of equal value.[4]

Today, we also find commentators, both non-Christian and Christian, arguing that rejection of the biblical worldview has catastrophic effects on Western culture. As Christian morality is rejected, sexual exploitation and abuse escalates.[5] Communities suffer when individual rights are elevated at the cost of service to others.[6] We all suffer when we're fragmented into competing identity groups[7] and trained to spot aggression (sexism, racism, homophobia, transphobia, ableism) in every social interaction.[8] Innocent people can be terrified of ending up on the wrong side of a zealous inquisition if they say the wrong thing about others' identity.[9]

The Christian way is a better way. At the core of the biblical worldview is commitment to serve others. The Christian God is a self-giving God. Jesus came "not to be served, but to serve, and to give his life as a ransom for many" (Mark 10:45). Moreover, Scripture commands Christians to love family, neighbors, strangers, and enemies. When true followers of Christ have obeyed these commands, they've challenged injustice and abuse and provided care for the needy. This has had beneficial effects on all areas of life—real freedom, flourishing, and fulfillment. Isn't that what we all want?

Freedom

Early in 1972, Paul Raffaele was wandering along a street in Canton, China, when he noticed a silent crowd surrounding an open truck. On it stood four men, heads bowed. Each had a board strapped to his back bearing his name—crossed out. Condemned to death, paraded round the streets as a warning to others before their execution, the men were victims of a tyrannical regime that attempted to control the actions and thoughts of a billion people. Dissent under that regime could lead to imprisonment, torture, or execution.[10]

If we live in the West, we often take freedom for granted. But the idea that every human is of equal dignity and should be afforded liberty has not been obvious to most cultures. Greco-Roman society had no concept that every human life has intrinsic value and dignity.[11] Human life was cheap.[12] The Roman Empire was made up of around seventy million people. Ten million of those were slaves. In fact, most societies throughout history have been built on slavery.[13] In some Islamic countries today, slavery still exists.[14] Today there are believed to be more slaves in the world than ever before: an estimated 27.6 million are victims of sex trafficking and forced labor.[15] Why has this been the norm?

Freedom Attacked in a Godless World

Pagan polytheists saw humanity and its destiny as in the hands of a capricious pantheon. The theory of evolution and the resulting naturalistic worldview sees humans as a product of chance in an impersonal universe. If we *are* just fated by the gods or the chance products of nature, there is no intrinsic value or dignity to every human life. When the true God and what his word says about human dignity are denied, oppressive rulers have no accountability to hold them in check.[16] All too often the state becomes God. For Karl Marx (1818–1883), for example, enslavement, torture, and killing could all be justified if they advanced the revolution.[17]

The author Aleksandr Solzhenitsyn (1918–2008) endured eight years in a Soviet labor camp. One night, he overheard the pitiful cries of a teenage girl. She'd dared to make *one* comment about freedom. She had to be punished so she would never think such dangerous things again.

> She . . . has already been standing in the wind for hours, her arms straight down, her head drooping, weeping, then growing numb and still. And then again she begs piteously: "Citizen Chief! Please forgive me! I won't do it again."
>
> The wind carries her moan to me, just as if she were moaning next to my ear.[18]

As Solzhenitsyn heard her cries, he vowed, "The whole world will read about you, girl!" Later, reflecting on the ideology that inflicted limitless suffering and killed around 148 million people,[19] he simply commented, "Men have forgotten God."[20]

Freedom: The Christian Foundation

The idea of human rights is founded on the biblical view that all people are created in God's image (Gen. 1:26–27).[21] This is what gives *every* individual *equal* dignity. When we see a fellow human being, we see someone who represents God himself; someone "crowned . . . with glory and honor" (Ps. 8:5). When we neglect or despise a fellow human being, we insult God. The sage says,

> Whoever oppresses the poor man insults his
>   Maker,
>   but he who is generous to the needy honors
>   him. (Prov. 14:31)

Supremely, Christians affirm the dignity of all human life because God himself, in Christ, became flesh, from the moment of conception. Christians also believe that every human life, from conception to natural death, should be protected,[22] because God, the giver of life, will judge the shedding of innocent blood (Gen. 9:6; Prov. 14:31). Every human is given a conscience (Rom. 2:15). God's moral law applies to ruler and ruled alike: all will give account to him (Rom. 13:1–4).

These biblical truths have been the foundation for the "rule of law" and our regard for human dignity and freedom. They've also inspired resistance to tyranny.[23] They form the only sure defense against the overweening, totalitarian claims of an all-powerful state.

Religious Freedom: Rooted in Biblical Truth

Belief in freedom of thought, religion, and speech goes back to a Christian understanding of creation as well. Those made in God's image have the God-given capacity to worship, love, and relate. Genuine worship, love, and relationship cannot be coerced. Liberty of conscience is a natural right that belongs to all God's image bearers.[24]

But through the centuries, sadly, there *were* times when the institutional church engaged in religious persecution and intolerance. This was an appalling perversion of biblical teaching.[25] Over those same centuries many Christians insisted that faith must be free, not forced. North African theologian Tertullian (ca. 155–ca. 220) insisted that persecution never results in genuine devotion: "Not even a human being would like to be honored unwillingly."[26] Similarly, Lactantius (ca. 250–ca. 325), another theologian from North Africa, argued: "If you want to defend religion by bloodshed, torture and evil . . . it will be polluted and outraged. There's nothing that is so much a matter of willingness as religion."[27] A landmark biblical defense of religious freedom was written in 1644 by American colonist Roger Williams, who had left England for Massachusetts to flee religious persecution in 1631.

Williams argued that forced worship is abominable to God, and that the magistrate has no place in controlling the church.[28]

Still today, Christians play a disproportionately large role in advancing religious freedom as a universal right,[29] including the freedom to change religion voluntarily.[30] This is despite the fact that in more than fifty countries, Christians themselves suffer high levels of persecution.[31]

On May 12, 2022, Deborah Yakubu, a second-year education student in Sokoto, Nigeria, was overjoyed that she'd passed an important exam. She posted a message on her WhatsApp discussion group, thanking Jesus for helping her. That enraged some of her classmates, who accused Deborah of insulting the prophet Muhammad. Deborah fled to a safe room but was pulled out and beaten to death with sticks. Her last words were, "What do you hope to achieve with this?"[32] She was one of thousands of Christians killed for their faith in Nigeria in the past two years.[33]

In the West, Christians don't face physical persecution, but they *are* under growing pressure to compromise their beliefs. In 2020, a class of students in Nevada was told that those who identified as Christian (or as white, or both) had to "undo and unlearn" their "beliefs, attitudes, and behaviors that stem from oppression." William Clark, the one biracial student in the class, didn't want to "unlearn" his Christianity[34] and refused to comply. He was not allowed to graduate.[35]

Christian Opposition to Slavery in History

The conviction that every human is made in God's image stood in stark contradiction to the culture of the ancient world.[36] The apostolic witness that in Christ we are all one, whether slave or free (Gal. 3:28) was revolutionary. For free people and slaves to share the Lord's Supper as fellow church members was scandalous. No other associations or pagan cults allowed slave and free to participate on an equal footing.

Chrysostom (ca. 347–407), who served as archbishop of Constantinople, was famous for his fearless denunciation of political leaders who abused their power. Nicknamed "Golden-Mouthed" because of his eloquent preaching, he told the wealthy to buy slaves, teach them a trade, and then set them free, saying that when Christ came he annulled slavery.[37]

Gregory of Nyssa (ca. 335–ca. 395) was another early church theologian who castigated abusive rulers. He wrote the first comprehensive critique of slavery, attacking it for its violation of the free nature of human beings made in God's image.[38]

It took time to root out slavery in the Western world, but Christian teaching and practice paved the way for arguing that as part of the body of Christ, slaves should be freed. By the eleventh century, slavery in Christendom had effectively ended.

The transatlantic slave trade brought back the horror on a more terrible scale. Christian campaigners worked tirelessly for its abolition, supported by vast numbers of evangelical Christians at a grassroots level. The British abolished the slave trade in 1807, and slavery itself in 1833. Shockingly, slavery continued in America for a further thirty years, and while some who claimed Christ supported it, many Christians, including many ex-slaves, resisted and sacrificially organized the Underground Railroad to facilitate slaves' escape. These abolitionists were willing to die for their conviction that we all descended from the same first parents, we are all made in God's image, we all have equal value, and we all bear a real responsibility to defend the freedom of our fellow human beings.

Christians Lead Opposition to Slavery Today

Little Bindya was born in the red-light district of the economic hub of India, Mumbai, where countless women are entrapped in prostitution. Bindya's mother died of HIV, and Bindya was rescued by a Christian rehabilitation center that helps women and girls leave prostitution and break the cycle of sex slavery and trafficking. By the age of fifteen, Bindya was top of her class at school, with hope of a meaningful future far from the red-light district.[39] Her life has been transformed for the better by the Christian gospel.

Bindya's story is just one example of how Christians today lead the way in opposing slavery and human trafficking worldwide. The International Justice Mission is one Christian network fighting abuse, but there are many others. Countless Christians devote their lives to rescuing and rehabilitating the victims of this appalling trade. Others support these endeavors with finances and prayer.

Missions and Freedom

The Bible commands Christians to care for the poor and oppressed, and to challenge injustice and discrimination (Lev. 19:15; Prov.17:15; Isa.1:17). In a fallen world the powerful and strong *do* often oppress the weak, and sometimes they use societal structures to do so. But throughout history, and around the world today, Christians have challenged abuse and worked for reform.

A research project of many years' duration showed that the greater the effects of Christian mission, the more likely governments are to respect human rights and the rule of law, and the less prone they are to tyranny.[40] Recent research demonstrates that

> proselytizing or conversionary Protestant missionaries heavily influenced the rise and spread of stable democracy around the world. . . . Such missionaries were a crucial catalyst initiating the development and spread of religious liberty, mass education, mass printing, newspapers, voluntary organisations and colonial reforms, thereby creating the conditions that made stable democracy more likely.[41]

All this laid the way for democracy. Missionaries campaigned against abuses of indigenous peoples, pushed for abolition of slavery in all British colonies, and were instrumental in ending the exploitative European opium trade in China.[42] Individual freedom and rights are most prevalent where Christianity has had the greatest effects.[43]

A Higher Throne

Christians insist that Jesus is Lord (Rom. 10:9; 1 Cor. 12:3). We should "render to Caesar the things that are Caesar's" (Mark 12:17), but ultimate obedience belongs to God, who stands above all earthly powers (Matt. 10:26–28).

Martin Niemöller (1892–1984), a Lutheran pastor in Germany, was imprisoned between 1938 and 1945 for his opposition to the Nazi regime. On one occasion, when interrogated by Hitler himself, Niemöller responded, "You can imprison me and you can torture me and you can kill me, but . . . one day you will give an account to one who is the King of kings and the Lord of lords."[44] Justice may not always be done in this life. But there will be a judgment, and justice *will* be done.

Think back to those condemned men paraded round the streets of Canton. They were just four among countless victims with no hope of a fair trial. But the King above all kings hears the cries of all the oppressed. He will hold all persecutors to account. And today, worldwide, Christians continue to insist that every human being has dignity because each one is created in God's image. That's the only solid basis for believing in justice and freedom for all. But freedom isn't the only benefit of the Christian faith. Christianity has also led to human flourishing through advances in areas such as philanthropy, healthcare, and education.

Flourishing

"The city resounds with weeping because of the numbers that have died and are dying every day," wrote Eusebius (ca. 260–ca. 340), bishop of Caesarea.[45]

It was the mid-third century. A hideous plague had reduced the population of the great North African city of Alexandria from half a million to less than two hundred thousand. Multitudes fled the city, often leaving their nearest and dearest to perish. The Christians were different.

> Heedless of danger, they took charge of the sick, attending to their every need and ministering to them in Christ, and with them departed this life

serenely happy; for they were infected by others with the disease, drawing on themselves the sickness of their neighbours.[46]

Believers cared not only for their own but also for neighbors and strangers. Many Christians contracted the plague and died horrible and lingering deaths. Their heroic service won widespread praise. Many pagans turned to Christ. These Alexandrian believers were true followers of Jesus, who came not to be served but to serve and to willingly give up his life for others (Matt. 20:28)—the one who commanded his followers to clothe the naked, feed the hungry, and care for the sick (Matt. 25:35–36).

Christians are often accused of being blind to suffering and injustice in this life because they fixate on happiness in the next. "Too heavenly minded to be any earthly use!" "Pie in the sky when you die!" scoff their opponents. But those who are *most* assured of heaven are often *most* willing to risk death in the service of others. Throughout history, and across the world today, Christians have led the way in philanthropy, healthcare, education, and efforts to relieve poverty.

Compassion: A Revolutionary Concept

In classical times, lavish giving to fund public projects was praised, but generosity was primarily seen as a way to flaunt the wealth and honor of the giver. To show pity for the poor and the weak was regarded as foolish sentimentality.

In this cultural context, the compassion shown by followers of Christ was revolutionary. Care for widows, orphans, the sick, the imprisoned, and the poor was viewed as essential to discipleship.[47] The Roman emperor Julian the Apostate (r. 361–363), who hated Christianity, believed that the Christians' sacrificial kindness toward strangers was a major factor in the spread of their beliefs: "It is a disgrace that these impious Galilaeans care not only for their own poor but for ours as well."[48]

In later times, Christians pioneered the establishment of hospitals, orphanages, leprosariums, and hospices for the dying.[49] During the Middle Ages both clergy and laity served in a wide range of ministries for the poor and the sick.[50] Hospitals were built by Christians throughout Western Europe.[51] Though monastic networks offering care to the sick and needy were dissolved in countries affected by the Reformation, Protestant clergy continued to demonstrate the Christian ethic of care.[52]

The Evangelical Awakenings of the eighteenth and nineteenth centuries affected whole nations, and as people found their lives transformed by Christ, they wanted to live out his words "As you did it to one of the least of these my brothers, you did it to me" (Matt. 25:40). Evangelical Christians were responsible for a remarkable range of social advance, including prison reform, care of the mentally ill, factory reform, rescuing women and children from sexual abuse, and provision of education. On a local level, mercy ministries and voluntary charitable societies flourished.

The Christian missionary movement of the nineteenth century also affected healthcare and philanthropy.

> Missionaries typically . . . opened the first hospitals and clinics, and pioneered Western medical education around the world. Informally many missionaries also taught hygiene and rudimentary medical knowledge and introduced new crops and livestock that improved the quality

of local diets. Thus, the historical prevalence of Protestant missionaries is associated with longer life expectancies and lower infant mortality rates.[53]

In *Half the Sky: How to Change the World*, Nicholas Kristof and Sheryl WuDunn document female oppression worldwide. The authors, liberal feminists, testify that when you travel to the poorest countries in Africa, you find aid workers around cities, but in the remote areas, where help is most needed, you find missionary doctors and church-sponsored aid workers. While aid workers and diplomats come and go, only the missionaries stay for life.[54] While secular liberals decry social injustice, they often merely lobby governments to give aid. Christians more often give generously themselves.[55]

Why? Jesus Christ promises, "Whoever seeks to preserve his life will lose it, but whoever loses his life will keep it" (Luke 17:33). We are not just living for the here and now. Death is not the end. We have the certain hope of resurrection and an eternity of enjoying God and community with all his people. We can afford to give our lives in service of others.

Lifting Nations from Poverty: Education

Vishal Mangalwadi was born in India in 1949. When he set out to read the holy books of his own nation, he found that they were not translated into the languages of the ordinary people. The Bible was. When he read it, he found that a central theme is God's desire to bless *all* nations. He decided to investigate whether the Bible had brought blessing to India. He found that many of the benefits enjoyed by modern Indians, such as their written languages, political democracy, and educational system, had been secured by Christian missionaries. Mangalwadi has also studied the influence of the Bible worldwide. He explains, "Western missions . . . birthed, financed, and nurtured hundreds of universities, thousands of colleges, and tens of thousands of schools. They educated millions and transformed nations."[56]

Living standards are raised when people apply their God-given reason to innovate, work, and solve problems. Education is essential to this process. Knowledge must be passed from one generation to the next to build on the achievements of the past.

From the inception of Christianity, education was a priority. After all, Christians believe that all human beings, made in God's image, should learn of God's works and ways. All should be able to read God's word in their own languages. All should develop skills to serve others for God's glory.

As a result of this priority, the earliest universities had Christian foundations. Perhaps more surprising for many, the biblical worldview even lay behind the development of the scientific method. It's rooted in the Christian conviction that God created the universe according to rational laws and endowed humans with the reason and intellect to study and explore.

Christians have also pioneered female education in many nations.[57] When you look at the markers of female oppression—whether child marriage, prostitution, sex trafficking, domestic violence, genital cutting, or so-called honor killing—all are more likely when girls are denied education. Christian advocacy for education has been key to liberating women from abuse, and essential for lifting communities out of poverty.

Lifting Nations from Poverty: Technology and Science

In ancient Egypt, engineers were capable of building vast pyramids, but they never thought to make wheelbarrows to make jobs easier for the slaves.[58] During the Middle Ages, laborsaving machines were developed in Christian monasteries because of the biblical teaching on human dignity and a reluctance to subject people to unnecessary toil.[59] Christian convictions lay behind the astonishing range of agricultural improvements, technological developments, and scientific experimentation in Europe. Waterwheels, fish farms, horseshoes, three-field crop rotation, eyeglasses, and numerous other innovations improved life for many.[60]

Norman Borlaug (1914–2009), grew up in poverty. He knew what it felt like to go to bed hungry.[61] Motivated by his Christian faith and deep compassion, Borlaug has been credited with saving more than a billion lives through his agricultural innovations, which have increased wheat yields over 700 percent. A Nobel Peace Prize–winning agronomist, Borlaug advised governments on economic policies to ensure that the food could be grown and would be available to their populations.

In a sinful world, we're all prone to greed. On a personal level we should guard against selfish consumerism, and the Bible condemns exploitation of others. But it remains true that the use of our God-given capacities

offers the best solution to world poverty and other chal-
lenges to human well-being. The only way to lift nations
out of poverty is for them to increase their production of
goods and services, for enterprise to be encouraged and
facilitated. Through efforts of Christians like Borlaug (as
well as other men and women influenced by a Christian
vision of compassion), global poverty has dramatically
decreased over the past two hundred years, even during
a time of enormous population growth.

What about the Environment?

God created this world as his beautiful domain, and he
set our first parents as his image bearers to manage it for
him. Adam and Eve were placed in a garden, and he commanded them to cultivate it. The rest of the earth was, as
yet, untamed: they were to "fill" and "subdue" it (Gen.
1:28). God gave them stewardship over the inanimate
creation (minerals, plants, forests), and dominion over
animate creation (animals, fish, birds). Nature would
reach its potential only by means of human cultivation.
Developing the rich resources God placed on earth would
involve innovations in agriculture, horticulture, animal
husbandry, science, technology, and much else.[62] After the

fall into sin (Gen. 3), the thorns and thistles that hindered productivity would need to be subdued.

Christians believe that responsible stewards don't unnecessarily spoil the resources with which they've been entrusted. We are to develop the earth for human blessing, but it must be managed wisely with a view to future generations.[63] God expects all people to treat other living things with care and consideration (Deut. 25:4; Prov. 12:10). This is why eighteenth-century evangelicals initiated the first society for the prevention of cruelty to animals.[64]

Human Flourishing

Western civilization was built on the biblical worldview and its respect for the individual as created in God's image, the belief that rulers are accountable to God, and the creation patterns of family and work. Unprecedented numbers of people across the globe were liberated from the grinding poverty of subsistence economies. Wealth creation was made possible by encouraged innovation, as well as the Christian work ethic.[65]

In a world of individuals who vary in competence and motivation, exact equality of outcomes cannot be attained without oppressive social engineering. But in countries influenced by the Christian worldview, inequalities have been mitigated as virtues of generosity, compassion, and social responsibility have been exercised and injustices have been addressed by a variety of reform movements.

Across the centuries and around the world, followers of Christ have devoted themselves to their neighbors' good. Their various endeavors—in healthcare, philanthropy, education, and everyday work—have been driven by the biblical conviction that humans, created in God's image, should *all* have opportunity to flourish. Every effort should be made to alleviate suffering, poverty, and need.

Human Flourishing Threatened in
a Post-Christian World

During the eighteenth century, promoters of the secular enlightenment in France ushered in the "age of reason." "Superstitions" associated with religion were to be left behind in history. All would then enjoy "Liberty, Equality, Fraternity!" The dream soon unraveled into a nightmare. During the Reign of Terror, forty thousand were brutally executed, living standards were knocked back, and educational provision for the poor withered as church schools were shut.

The twentieth century witnessed even more disastrous efforts to impose equal outcomes on whole nations. Atheistic Marxism

> left in its wake an economic, environmental, social, and cultural disaster. . . . [It] usually made living conditions worse than before the revolution. . . . Almost 55 million people died in various Marxist famines and associated epidemics [mostly as] an unintended result of Marxist collectivization and agricultural policies.[66]

As I write, we are rightly outraged by the loss of life, perhaps numbering tens of thousands, caused by the Russian invasion of Ukraine.[67] But many forget that *millions* of Ukrainians were starved and slaughtered between 1930 and 1933 during the great famine caused by Stalin's agricultural "reforms."[68]

From a Culture of Life to a Culture of Death

In 1920, a book entitled *Allowing the Destruction of Life Unworthy of Life* was published in Germany.[69] Those with brain injuries, intellectual disabilities, and psychiatric illnesses were described as having lives not worth extending. Eliminating them was seen as humane. Under Hitler, that belief would be applied with grotesque effect. Have we fully progressed past these horrors?

Today in many Western countries, most view humankind as only the product of random mutation and natural selection. If this is the case, then the idea of the sanctity of every human life—the logic of protecting it above animal life or the environment[70]—can be relegated to history, and medical ethics will collapse into relativism.

In 1992, a majority of US Supreme Court justices ruled that "at the heart of liberty is the right to *define one's own concept* of existence, of meaning, of the universe, and *of the mystery of human life*."[71] That implies that *we*, not God, decide *when* human life begins and *which* lives are worth protecting. So, worldwide, 73 million unborn children are killed every year.[72] Increasing numbers of countries allow assisted suicide or euthanasia. In Canada, the poor and homeless have been offered medical help to die. It's cheaper to kill them than care for them.[73]

Finnish activist Pentti Linkola (1932–2020) goes further, arguing that humans consume too many of nature's resources. Most of us should be killed, and the remainder controlled by an authoritarian environmentalist state, with strict controls on procreation.[74] Environmental activist Greta Thunberg (b. 2003) calls for the overthrow of the entire capitalist system. No matter that it has led to raising the average life expectancy worldwide from thirty years to seventy years.[75] The environment is more important than mere human flourishing.[76]

These examples show that when God's truth is denied, the individual and societal effects are disastrous. The truth about God and about human beings as revealed in nature and Scripture is the only solid foundation for the protection of human life, dignity, and flourishing.[77]

In 1976, Vishal Mangalwadi and his wife, Ruth, started a nonprofit organization to serve the rural poor in Central India. When they tried to save the life of their neighbor's child, the parents resisted all their efforts. Little Sheela was starved to death because she was regarded as a liability.[78] In that culture, female infanticide was commonplace. The Mangalwadi's neighbors couldn't comprehend why Vishal and Ruth wanted to save Sheela's life:

Three thousand years of Hinduism, twenty-six hundred years of Buddhism, a thousand years of Islam, and a century of secularism had collectively failed to give them a convincing basis for recognizing and affirming the unique value of a human being.[79]

It's clear. Respect for every human life did not arise from the other world religions or from secularism. It arose from the biblical conviction that God created man and woman in his own image. That's the foundation for freedom, for flourishing, and also, as we'll see, for fulfillment.

Fulfillment

A century ago, Margaret Sanger, the founder of Planned Parenthood, published *The Pivot of Civilization*.[80] She was convinced that all misery and suffering were caused by the enforcement of Christian morality. She thought humans would experience happiness and "fulfillment" only if they enjoyed unlimited sexual freedom, and universal contraceptive provision would make that possible.

For Sanger and other pioneers of the sexual revolution, God (if he exists), is a cosmic killjoy. Many today agree.

They insist we can justify our own desires and shape our own identity. "Love is Love," and the only boundary is consent. A sexual revolution has transformed Western culture over the past century.

The First Sexual Revolution: From Darkness to Light

Two thousand years ago a different sexual revolution transformed the Roman Empire. It liberated millions from coercion and abuse. The Christian church was born at a time when a privileged elite of males had sexual access to the rest of the population.[81] The poorest men who did not have free access to their own slaves could hire prostitutes for pathetically low sums. Vile cruelty surrounded the sex trade. Forced abortion and infanticide compounded the suffering for women. Unlimited sexual freedom had only served the interests of the powerful and privileged. It was terrible for everyone else, and worst for women and children.

The Christian conviction that God is the giver of life meant that all human life was to be regarded as sacred, including unborn and newborn life. That worked for the protection of women as well as their children. The Christian sexual ethic forbade the buying and selling of sex. It held men and women to an equal standard: husbands and wives were to be faithful to each other (1 Cor. 7:1–4). Girls were not married off at a young age. Casual sexual exploitation, widespread abuse, shocking coercion, abortion, and infanticide were all challenged by biblical morality, and ultimately they were radically limited by legislation as well.

In AD 40, there were probably no more than a few thousand Christians in the Roman Empire. By 350, there may have been more than thirty-three million Christians out of a total population of sixty million.[82] A significant factor in that growth was the appeal of Christian ethics.

God's Design Works Best

God's moral law was codified in the Ten Commandments, and it is placed on every human heart by means of the conscience. The Bible commands marriage partners to be faithful to each other and children to honor their parents.[83] When these commands are upheld, families are protected. Lifelong marriages are good for children, for communities, and for society.[84] Stable families and communities, based on mutual fidelity and service, provide the context for lasting fulfillment.

The Second Sexual Revolution: Back into the Darkness

Today we live on the wrong side of the second sexual revolution. The "new morality" prevailing in Western culture has reversed the Christian moral code.

The "natural" family of a married father and mother was once accepted as the fundamental building block of society; it's now often thought to be a seedbed of abuse and an outdated relic of heteronormativity. Sexual freedom used to be regarded as sinful; it's now seen as healthy. Modesty, chastity, and sexual restraint used to be considered virtues; they're now viewed as pathological. Sexual activity was to be limited to within marriage (this precluded children from sexual activity); children are now seen as entitled to sexual pleasure. Fulfilling our own "sexual orientation," living according to our own unique "gender identity," and unlimited access to abortion are all regarded as nonnegotiable human rights. The sex-positive movement encourages unlimited (consensual) sexual pleasure as healthy.

It's not working well.

When the guardrails of God's moral law are smashed down, the consequences are catastrophic on an individual level. Margaret Sanger devoted her life to the abolition of Christian morality and the promotion of sexual liberation. But her own life was a mess: failed marriages, neglected children, numerous affairs, attempts to cover up her complicity with the Nazi regime, and desperate attempts to find meaning via occult activities.[85]

The consequences are catastrophic on a societal level as well. Feminist Louise Perry[86] has worked with victims of rape and abuse. She has seen the dark side of radical feminism and sexual liberation. Young women are told that casual sex is empowering. They are the losers in a hook-up culture, which delivers loveless sex, humiliating abuse, and miserable abandonment. While there are individual exceptions, on average, women and children are safer within the married family than anywhere else.[87] Monogamous, faithful, lifelong marriage is good for men, women, children, and all society.[88]

Children Betrayed

Pioneers of sexual liberation such as Sanger and Alfred Kinsey insisted that children are capable of sexual pleasure and have a "right" to engage in sexual activity.[89] Sadly, their ideas unleashed a tsunami of sexual exploitation.

La Familia Grande, a best-selling memoir by Camille Kouchner, describes the incest and abuse that pervaded the top echelons of French intellectual society during the permissive 1960s and '70s. Camille's stepdad (a respected Paris intellectual) taught her that "allowed" and "forbidden" were purely personal choices.[90] But his "personal choice" was to abuse Camille's twin brother sexually, causing irrevocable damage.

French philosopher Michel Foucault (1926–1984) viewed moral codes as ways of oppressing the weak. He celebrated transgressiveness. He lived out liberation from moral norms himself, engaging in systematic sexual abuse of boys between ages eight and ten while living in North Africa.[91] He exploited others, even as he castigated others for doing likewise.

Today, sexual liberation fuels the global explosion of pornography, which sustains a web of abuse and people trafficking, even as it destroys intimate relationships and stable family life. Sex has been depersonalized and dehumanized. Many young people are told that sex is "just a recreational activity." But many end up feeling used, abused, and betrayed. Third-wave feminists argued that pornography can be empowering for women. But increasing evidence shows that it's dangerously addictive. It feeds a culture in which young girls are objectified daily.[92] Abuse has escalated in every context: in Hollywood,[93] among sports coaches,[94] and, as Sophie testified, from predators entering the church.

Freedom without boundaries ends up in dystopia, not utopia!

A Sure Foundation for Human Dignity

Far from feeling embarrassed about their faith, Christians need to be confident. The Christian worldview provides all of the following:

- The only solid foundation for *human dignity*. We have all been created in the image of God (Gen. 1:26–28).
- The only firm defense of *human unity*. We are all descended from the same first parents (Gen. 1:28; Acts 17:26).
- The only solid foundation for *real freedom*. No government has the authority to tell us what to think. We will each answer to God (Acts 5:29).
- The only solid foundation for *morality*. The perfectly just and righteous God has given every one of us a conscience, an awareness of his moral law (Rom. 2:15).

- The only sure way to *human flourishing*. Family, work, and civil authorities have been affected by sin, but they are God's provision for our good (Matt. 19:4–6; Rom.13:1–8; 1 Tim. 5:8).
- The only solid foundation for *future hope*. Death is not the end. Every human is of eternal significance. We will all be raised to new life. There will be a judgment when justice will be done. God's people will enjoy and serve him forever in the new heavens and new earth (1 Cor. 15; Rev. 21–22).

Think back to Sophie.

The very fact that she *is* outraged by abuse shows that the Creator God has given her—and each one of us—a conscience. We know there is such a thing as evil! We are created by God to care about cruelty and injustice. We are not biological or chemical accidents. Biological and chemical accidents don't care! As the atheistic regimes of the twentieth century demonstrated, societies from which Christian influence is eliminated are wretched places to live. And as Western society is discovering, societies that turn away from Christian morality are increasingly abusive and dangerous, especially for women and children.

When I was a history teacher, I explained to my students that the Christian worldview alone accounts for *both* the evil *and* the good in the world. Any thinking person has to be appalled at the suffering we witness daily on the news. But we also have to marvel at so much that is beautiful and good. The biblical worldview explains why we are in such a mess: we have sinned against our Creator. It also explains why we see such good in our fellow human beings: each one has been created in the image of God.

Christians grieve at the evil and suffering in the world, but we are confident that Jesus is Lord. He came into the world to "destroy the works of the devil" (1 John 3:8). That includes all brokenness of lives, all injustice in communities, all guilt, and all pain. His kingdom is extending through all nations. One day the world will be renewed, and his reign of perfect justice will prevail.

Right now, the line between good and evil runs right through every human heart. We all go against our God-given conscience. But Jesus Christ extends the offer of forgiveness to everyone without exception. "Whoever comes to me I will never cast out" (John 6:37), he says. "Come to me, all who labor and are heavy laden, and I will give you rest" (Matt. 11:28).

The glory of the biblical Christian message is that however messed up our lives may be, forgiveness is offered as a gift of grace. Every other religion (including false Christianity) tells us to "be good" in order to get to heaven.

Bhaskar Rao grew up in a high-class, devout Hindu family in India. His granddad was a holy man who knew the Hindu scriptures by heart and performed all the correct rituals. Bhaskar loved him dearly. But when his granddad fell ill, the old man had no peace and died in terror of what would come next. Bhaskar concluded that his religion offered no hope. He decided to commit suicide but, "by chance," heard someone preaching the gospel. He was stunned by the promise: "Believe on the Lord Jesus Christ and *you will be saved* and have eternal life." He had never come across such certainty! He was converted, was baptized, and went on to share the gospel with others.[95] Bhaskar then found, as so many others have, that when the Holy Spirit works in a person to break the chains of sin and self, we are empowered to live for God's glory and the good of neighbor (Titus 2:14).

That's why Christ's followers through the centuries have willingly served others. They have also proclaimed the gospel, even when it has cost them their lives. Countless individuals have found their lives transformed for the better as a result. Across the globe and across the centuries, where living Christianity has spread, we find lives changed and communities transformed. It really is good news for the whole world.

Notes

1. "Atheism Doubles among Generation Z," Barna, January 24, 2018, https://www.barna.com/.

2. Tom Holland, *Dominion: The Making of the Western Mind* (London: Little, Brown, 2019), xxvii.

3. Holland, *Dominion*, 523.

4. Tom Holland, "Why I Was Wrong about Christianity," *New Statesman*, September 14, 2016, https://www.new statesman.com/. Other commentators arguing for the positive impact of the biblical worldview especially in the culture of the West include Jordan Peterson and Douglas Murray.

5. Louise Perry, *The Case against the Sexual Revolution: A New Guide to Sex in the 21st Century* (London: Polity, 2022).

6. Patrick J. Deneen, *Why Liberalism Failed* (New Haven, CT: Yale University Press, 2018), 176–77.

7. Mark Lilla, *The Once and Future Liberal: After Identity Politics* (New York: HarperCollins, 2017), 10–12. See also Douglas Murray, *The Madness of Crowds: Gender, Race and Identity* (London: Bloomsbury, 2019); Joshua Mitchell, *American Awakening: Identity Politics and Other Afflictions of Our Time* (New York: Encounter, 2022).

8. Helen Pluckrose and James Lindsay, *Cynical Theories: How Universities Made Everything about Race, Gender, and Identity—and Why This Harms Everybody* (London: Swift, 2020).

9. John McWhorter, *Woke Racism: How a New Religion Has Betrayed Black America* (New York: Portfolio/Penguin, 2021), 5.

10. Paul Raffaele, "The Masses Might Even Stone You," *Critic*, June 1, 2021, https://thecritic.co.uk/.

11. Gary D. Ferngren, *Medicine and Healthcare in Early Christianity* (Baltimore: Johns Hopkins University Press, 2009), 95–96.

12. Rodney Stark, *For the Glory of God: How Monotheism Led to Reformations, Science, Witch-Hunts, and the End of Slavery* (Princeton, NJ: Princeton University Press, 2004), 291.

13. Sheldon. M. Stern, "The Atlantic Slave Trade: The Full Story," *Academic Questions* 18, no. 3 (2005): 17, https://eric.ed.gov/; Thomas Sowell, "The Real History of Slavery," in *Black Rednecks and White Liberals* (New York: Encounter, 2005), 112–13, 156–58.

14. Paul Raffaele, "How the World Turns a Blind Eye to African Slavery," *Critic*, November 2022, https://thecritic.co.uk/.

15. Virginia Allen, "Root Cause of Human Trafficking Is 'Individuals Who Decide to Exploit' Vulnerable People, Expert Says," *Daily Signal*, December 8, 2022, https://www.dailysignal.com/2022/12/08/root-cause-of-human-trafficking-individuals-who-decide-to-exploit-vulnerable-people-expert-says/.

16. The principle that the ruler is not above the law was enshrined in *Magna Carta* in 1215. It was based on biblical foundations (1 Kings 21; Rom. 13:1).

17. Professor Wilfred Cantwell Smith, *Islam in Modern History* (1957), cited by Dennis Prager and Joseph Telushkin, *The Nine Questions People Ask about Judaism* (New York: Simon & Schuster, 1986), 92.

18. Aleksandr I. Solzhenitsyn, *The Gulag Archipelago, 1918–1956: An Experiment in Literary Investigation*, trans.

Thomas P. Whitney, vol. 2 (New York: Harper and Row, 1975), 147–48.

19. R. J. Rummel, "The Killing Machine That Is Marxism," *Schwarz Report*, December 15, 2004, https://www.schwarzreport.org/resources/essays/the-killing-machine-that-is-marxism.

20. Aleksandr Solzhenitsyn, "Men Have Forgotten God: Aleksandr Solzhenitsyn's 1983 Templeton Address," *National Review*, December 11, 2018, https://www.nationalreview.com/.

21. Tom Holland comments, "If there is a single wellspring for the reverence they [secular humanists] display towards their own species, it is the opening chapter of the Bible." "Humanism Is a Heresy," *UnHerd* (blog), November 26, 2022, https://unherd.com/.

22. John R. Ling, *When Does Human Life Begin? Christian Thinking and Contemporary Opposition* (n.p.: Christian Institute, 2017), 7; https://www.christian.org.uk/wp-content/uploads/when-does-human-life-begin.pdf.

23. Vishal Mangalwadi, *The Book That Made Your World: How the Bible Created the Soul of Western Civilization* (Nashville: Thomas Nelson, 2011), 334–54.

24. Andrew Walker, "The Imago Dei and Religious Liberty," in *Liberty for All: Defending Everyone's Religious Freedom in a Pluralistic Age* (Grand Rapids, MI: Brazos, 2021), 81–110.

25. This biblical principle of religious liberty was undermined, and all too often forgotten, during the "sacral" era. This was the period of history when it was assumed that a territory had to have a single faith. It was thought that there would be disorder and fragmentation if that unity were undermined. The terrible outcome of that was the persecution of dissenters. However, descriptions of both the Inquisition and the Crusades have often been exaggerated. See Rodney Stark, *Bearing False Witness: Debunking Centuries of Anti-Catholic History* (London: SPCK, 2017); and Stark, *God's Battalions: The Case for the Crusades* (New York: HarperOne, 2009).

26. Tertullian, *Apology* 24, quoted in Robert L. Wilken, *Liberty in the Things of God: The Christian Origins of Religious Freedom* (New Haven, CT: Yale University Press, 2019), 11.

27. Lactantius, *Divine Institutes* 5.19, 23, quoted in *Christianity and Freedom*, vol. 1, *Historical Perspectives*, ed. Timothy Samuel Shah and Allen D. Hertzke (Cambridge: Cambridge University Press, 2016), 9–10.

28. Roger Williams, *The Bloudy Tenent of Persecution for Cause of Conscience* (1644), Online Library of Liberty, https://oll.libertyfund.org/pages/1644-williams-bloody -tenet-of-persecution-letter.

29. Allen D. Hertzke, "Christianity and Freedom in the Contemporary World," in *Christianity and Freedom*, vol. 2, *Contemporary Perspectives*, ed. Allen D. Hertzke and Timothy Samuel Shah (Cambridge: Cambridge University Press, 2016), 4, 11.

30. "A state that hinders conversion is uncivilised because it restricts the human quest for truth and reform." Vishal and Ruth Mangalwadi, *Carey, Christ, and Cultural Transformation: The Life and Influence of William Carey* (Carlisle, UK: OM, 1993), 67.

31. "World Watch List 2023," Open Doors, https://www .opendoorsuk.org/persecution/.

32. Campbell Campbell-Jack, "Deborah Thanked Jesus for Helping Her in an Exam," The Conservative Woman, May 23,2022, https://www.conservative woman.co.uk/.

33. Caroline Cox, "The West Should Recognise the Genocide of Nigeria's Christians," Conservative Home, November 22, 2022, https://conservativehome.com/.

34. Valerie Edwards, "Bi-racial High School Senior Who Looks White Is Failed after Refusing to Confess 'White Dominance' and 'Attach Derogatory Labels' to His Race, Gender, Religious and Sexual Identity," *Daily Mail*, March 11, 2021, https://www.dailymail.co.uk/news /article-9352639/Bi-racial-high-school-senior-looks -white-failed-refusing-confess-white-dominance.html.

35. William Clark and his mother, Gabrielle, have taken legal action to challenge that decision. They objected to the infringement of religious belief and to the overt racism of the course content. On November 16, 2020, their lawyer wrote to the school: "William's father, now deceased, is white. Gabrielle also has a white parent. As such they object to the glib racism of your course materials and program- ming, which includes statements in no apparent context like 'Racism is what white people do to people of color,' re- peated ad infinitum. This and statements like it are patently racist, create a hostile and divisive educational environ- ment, and violate Title VI of the Civil Rights Act." "Clark v. State Public Charter School Authority," Liberty Justice Center, December 23, 2020, https://libertyjusticecenter .org/cases/clark-v-state-public-charter-school-authority/. At the time of writing, the case has not yet been settled.

36. Jewish culture was distinctive. There was bonded labor, but with the recognition that all humans have dignity. It is unfortunate that the Hebrew word 'ebed (also transliterated as 'eved), which historically meant and had always been translated as "servant," is now often translated "slave" in modern language versions of the Bible. This gives a misleading impression of Jewish culture, as the word now carries a heavy freight of association with the horrors of plantation slavery. Peter J. Williams, "Does the Bible Condone Slavery?," BeThinking, 2015, https://www.bethinking.org/. See also Sowell, *Black Rednecks and White Liberals*, 111–69.

37. Chrysostom, "Homily 40 on First Corinthians," https://www.newadvent.org/.

38. David Bentley Hart, "The 'Whole Humanity': Gregory of Nyssa's Critique of Slavery in Light of His Eschatology," *Scottish Journal of Theology* 54, no. 1 (2001): 51–69; Kyle Harper, "Christianity and the Roots of Human Dignity in Late Antiquity," in Shah and Hertzke, *Christianity and Freedom*, 1:133–34.

39. Janet Weber, "Freeing the Dalits," OM, September 23, 2018, https://www.om.org/en/news/freeing-dalits.

40. Robert D. Woodberry, "Protestant Missionaries and the Centrality of Conversion Attempts for the Spread

of Education, Printing, Colonial Reform, and Political Democracy," in Shah and Hertzke, *Christianity and Freedom*, 1:367–90.

41. Robert D. Woodbury, quoted by Timothy Samuel Shah, "Christianity and Freedom: Ancient Roots and Historical Innovations," in Shah and Hertzke, *Christianity and Freedom*, 1:25.

42. Shah, "Christianity and Freedom," 26. It is wrong to dismiss missionaries as agents of political or cultural imperialism.

43. Woodberry, "Protestant Missionaries," 367–90.

44. David S. Dockery and Timothy George, *The Great Tradition of Christian Thinking: A Student's Guide*, Reclaiming the Christian Intellectual Tradition (Wheaton, IL: Crossway, 2012), 76.

45. Eusebius, *The History of the Church from Christ to Constantine*, trans. G. A. Williamson (New York: Dorset, 1984), 305.

46. Letter from Dionysius, in Eusebius, *The History of the Church*, 237, quoted in Rodney Stark, *The Rise of Christianity* (New York: HarperSanFrancisco, 1997), 76.

47. David Bentley Hart, *Atheist Delusions: The Christian Revolution and Its Fashionable Enemies* (New Haven, CT: Yale University Press, 2009), 164.

48. Julian, letter 22, to Arsacius, quoted in Hart, *Atheist Delusions*, 45.

49. Os Guinness, *Renaissance: The Power of the Gospel However Dark the Times* (Leicester, UK: Inter-Varsity Press, 2014), 26.

50. A. J. Davis, 'The Charitable Revolution," *Christian History*, 101 (2011), https://christianhistoryinstitute.org/.

51. Alvin J. Schmidt, *How Christianity Changed the World* (Grand Rapids, MI: Zondervan, 2004), 159.

52. Peter Saunders, "Medicine and the Reformation," *Triple Helix*, Autumn 2017, Christian Medical Fellowship, https://www.cmf.org.uk/.

53. Woodberry, "Protestant Missionaries," 385.

54. Nicholas D. Kristof and Sheryl WuDunn, *Half the Sky: Turning Oppression into Opportunity for Women Worldwide* (London: Virago, 2010), 157–60.

55. Kristof and WuDunn, *Half the Sky*, 160.

56. Mangalwadi, *The Book That Made Your World*, 207–8.

57. Sharon James, "Ann Judson and the Triumph of Female Education," TGC, November 14, 2022, https://www.thegospelcoalition.org/.

58. Mangalwadi, *The Book That Made Your World*, 93.

59. Mangalwadi, *The Book That Made Your World*, 95.

60. Hart, *Atheist Delusions*, 72–73.

61. Vijay Jayaraj, "I Was Hungry and You Fed Me: The Legacy of Norman Borlaug," *Christian Examiner*, June 17, 2016, https://www.christianexaminer.com/news/i-was-hungry-and-you-fed-me-the-legacy-of-norman-borlaug.html.

62. Anthony Hoekema, *Created in God's Image* (Grand Rapids, MI: Eerdmans, 1986), 79.

63. Arguably the worst instances of environmental destruction have occurred in Communist economies. Wayne Grudem and Barry Asmus, *The Poverty of Nations: A Sustainable Solution* (Wheaton, IL: Crossway, 2013), 250–52.

64. J. Wesley Bready, *England before and after Wesley* (London: Hodder and Stoughton, 1939), 150–55, 407–8.

65. "Free markets and growth necessary to lift people out of poverty." Jon Berkeley, "Towards the End of Poverty," *Economist*, June 1, 2013, https://www.economist.com/.

66. Rummel, "The Killing Machine That Is Marxism."

67. Fred Kelly, "Ukraine Death Toll: How Many People Have Died in the War?," *Week*, December 2, 2022, https://www.theweek.co.uk/.

68. Anne Applebaum, *Red Famine: Stalin's War on Ukraine* (New York: Anchor, 2018).

69. Karl Binding and Alfred Hoche, *Allowing the Destruction of Life Unworthy of Life*, trans. Cristina Modak (n.p.: Suzeteo Enterprises, 2012), https://lifeunworthy oflife.com.

70. Peter Singer, *Writings on an Ethical Life* (London: Fourth Estate, 2002), 35.

71. *Planned Parenthood of Southeastern Pa. v. Casey*, Justia, June 29, 1992, https://supreme.justia.com/cases/federal /us/505/833/, emphasis mine.

72. "Unintended Pregnancy and Abortion Worldwide," Guttmacher Institute, March 23, 2022, https://www .guttmacher.org/.

73. Kevin Yuill, "Canada's Euthanasia Laws Are a Moral Outrage," *Spiked*, November 17, 2022, https://www .spiked-online.com/.

74. See, for example, sentiments expressed in Pentti Linkola, "Humanflood," trans. Harri Heinonen and Michael Moynihan, 1989, http://www.penttilinkola.com/pentti _linkola/ecofascism_writings/humanflood/.

75. India McTaggart, "Greta Thunberg: It's Time to Transform the West's Oppressive and Racist Capitalist System," *Telegraph*, November 2, 2022, https://www .telegraph.co.uk/.

76. Human flourishing and environmental responsibility do not need to be pitted against each other. They work in harmony. Grudem and Asmus, *The Poverty of Nations*, 250–52.

77. Sharon James, "The 20th Century: A Case Study in Losing Human Dignity," TGC, March 3, 2022, thegospel-coalition.org/.

78. Mangalwadi, *The Book That Made Your World*, 63.

79. Mangalwadi, *The Book That Made Your World*, 72.

80. Margaret Sanger, *The Pivot of Civilization* (n.p.: 1922), https://gutenberg.org/.

81. Kyle Harper, *From Shame to Sin: The Christian Transformation of Sexual Morality in Late Antiquity* (Cambridge: Harvard University Press, 2016); Matthew Rueger, *Sexual Morality in a Christless World* (St. Louis, MO: Concordia, 2016).

82. Stark, *The Rise of Christianity*, 7.

83. Commandment 5, "Honor your father and your mother" (Ex. 20:12); Commandment 7, "You shall not commit adultery" (Ex. 20:14). Sexual activity outside marriage is prohibited, which rules out sexual activity with, for example, children. Daniel R. Heimbach, *True Sexual Morality: Recovering Biblical*

Standards for a Culture in Crisis (Wheaton, IL: Crossway, 2004), 194–95.

84. Kevin DeYoung, "What Should Christians Think about Same-Sex Marriage?," Crossway (website), November 28, 2022, https://www.crossway.org/articles/what-about-same-sex-marriage/; Mary Eberstadt, "The Fury of the Fatherless," *First Things*, December 2020, https://www.firstthings.com/.

85. George Grant, *Killer Angel: A Biography of Planned Parenthood's Founder Margaret Sanger* (Franklin, TN: Ars Vitae, 1995), chap. 10; Sharon James, "Margaret Sanger: Sex as Salvation," Christian Institute, August 6, 2020, https://www.christian.org.uk/.

86. Perry, *The Case against the Sexual Revolution.*

87. Sharon James, review of *The Case against the Sexual Revolution,* by Louise Perry, Affinity, November 9, 2022, https://www.affinity.org.uk/social-issues/book-review-the-case-against-the-sexual-revolution/.

88. "The American Family Survey: 2022 Report," Deseret News, https://www.deseret.com/american-family-survey. Stable marriage and family life are strongly linked to happiness and to personal mental health in particular.

89. Alfred Kinsey, a twentieth-century sexual researcher, claimed that from infancy, children were sexually active and should be encouraged to satisfy their desires. His "experiments" involved the abuse of infants and children. Kinsey, *Sexual Behaviour in the Human Male* (London: Saunders, 1948), 157–92.

90. Camille Kouchner, *The Familia Grande* (London: Brazen, 2022), 58. See also Agnes Poirier, "Camille Kouchner's Familia Grande: 'I Knew My Stepfather's Games . . . but with My Brother, Too?'" *Guardian*, May 14, 2022, https://www.theguardian.com/.

91. Jaythem Guesmi, "Reckoning with Foucault's Alleged Sexual Abuse of Boys in Tunisia," *Al Jazeera*, April 16, 2021, https://www.aljazeera.com/opinions/2021/4/16/reckoning-with-foucaults-sexual-abuse-of-boys-in-tunisia.

92. Becket Cook, "The Pornification of American Girls," *The Becket Cook Show* (podcast), Spotify, December 2021, https://open.spotify.com/episode/759vnfyxL5DCOGZwmWv1KZ.

93. The egregious abuse committed by Hollywood director Harvey Weinstein from the 1970s onward led to his conviction in 2020. It triggered the #MeToo

movement, which exposed abuse in numerous work-place and other settings.

94. Tom Lutz, "Report Finds Sexual Misconduct and Emotional Abuse Is 'Systemic' in US Women's Soccer," *Guardian*, October 3, 2022, https://www.theguardian.com/.

95. Dorothy Carswell, *Real Lives* (Carlisle, UK: Paternoster, 2001).

Recommended Resources

Cook, Becket. *A Change of Affection: A Gay Man's Incredible Story of Redemption*. Nashville: Thomas Nelson, 2019. A compelling testimony of how the gospel brings liberation and fulfillment.

Grudem, Wayne, and Barry Asmus. *The Poverty of Nations: A Sustainable Solution*. Wheaton, IL: Crossway, 2013. A powerful explanation of how following the biblical worldview results in human flourishing.

James, Sharon. *How Christianity Transformed the World*. Fearn, Ross-shire, UK: Christian Focus, 2021. An overview of the impact of Christianity on areas such as freedom, justice, education, healthcare, philanthropy, and the dignity of women.

James, Sharon. *The Lies We Are Told: The Truth We Must Hold*. Fearn, Ross-shire, UK: Christian Focus, 2022.

An overview of how, in practice, the outworking of non-Christian worldviews has a catastrophic effect at both individual and societal levels.

James, Sharon. *A Student's Guide to Worldview*. Fearn, Ross-shire, UK: Christian Focus, 2022. A brief summary of how the biblical worldview compares with current non-Christian claims.

Mangalwadi, Vishal. *The Book That Made Your World: How the Bible Created the Soul of Western Civilization*. Nashville: Thomas Nelson, 2011. A survey of the global impact of the Bible.

Rueger, Matthew. *Sexual Morality in a Christless World*. St. Louis, MO: Concordia, 2016. A survey of the negative impact of unlimited sexual freedom in the ancient world and today.

Scripture Index

Genesis

1:26–27 6
1:26–28 35
1:28 . . . . 23, 35
3 24
9:6 7

Exodus

20:12 . . . . 53n83
20:14 . . . . 53n83

Leviticus

19:15 12

Deuteronomy

25:4 24

1 Kings

21 . . . . 43n16

Psalms

8:5 7

Proverbs

12:10 24
14:31 7
17:15 12

Isaiah

1:17 12

Matthew

7:16 2
10:26–28 14
11:28 37
18:6 1
19:4–6 36
20:28 16
25:35–36 16
25:40 18

Mark

10:45 3
12:17 14

Luke
17:33.................19

John
6:37..................37

Acts
5:29..................35
17:26.................35

Romans
2:15..................7, 35
10:9..................14
13:1..................43n16
13:1–4...............7
13:1–8...............36

1 Corinthians
7:1–4................31
12:3..................14
15....................36

Galatians
3:28..................10

1 Timothy
5:8...................36

Titus
2:14..................38

1 John
3:8...................37

Revelation
21–22................36

TGC THE GOSPEL COALITION

The Gospel Coalition (TGC) supports the church in making disciples of all nations, by providing gospel-centered resources that are trusted and timely, winsome and wise.

Guided by a Council of more than 40 pastors in the Reformed tradition, TGC seeks to advance gospel-centered ministry for the next generation by producing content (including articles, podcasts, videos, courses, and books) and convening leaders (including conferences, virtual events, training, and regional chapters).

In all of this we want to help Christians around the world better grasp the gospel of Jesus Christ and apply it to all of life in the 21st century. We want to offer biblical truth in an era of great confusion. We want to offer gospel-centered hope for the searching.

Join us by visiting TGC.org so you can be equipped to love God with all your heart, soul, mind, and strength, and to love your neighbor as yourself.

TGC.org

TGC Hard Questions Series

Does God Care about Gender Identity?

Samuel D. Ferguson

Is Christianity Good for the World?

Sharon James

Why Do We Feel Lonely at Church?

Jeremy Linneman

TGC Hard Questions is a series of short booklets that seek to answer common but difficult questions people ask about Christianity. The series serves the church by providing tools that answer unchurched people's deep longings for community, their concerns about biblical ethics, and their doubts about confessional faith.

For more information, visit **crossway.org**.

Also Available from
the Gospel Coalition

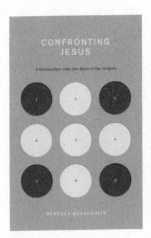
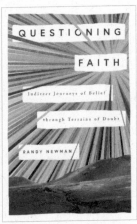

For more information, visit **crossway.org**.